BEST OF MARCH MADNESS

UNFORGETTABLE MOMENTS IN MARCH MADNESS

BY CHARLIE BEATTIE

abdobooks.com

Published by Abdo Publishing, a division of ABDO, PO Box 398166, Minneapolis, Minnesota 55439.

Printed in the United States of America, North Mankato, Minnesota.
102025
012026

Cover Photos: Streeter Lecka/Getty Images Sport/Getty Images, Ben Solomon/NCAA Photos/Getty Images, Amy Sancetta/AP Images
Interior Photos: Andy Lyons/Getty Images Sport/Getty Images, 4–5, 8, 35; Tony Gutierrez/AP Images, 6; Pete Leabo/AP Images, 10–11; Matthew Stockman/Allsport/Getty Images Sport/Getty Images, 13; Ronald Martinez/Getty Images Sport/Getty Images, 15; Danny Moloshok/AP Images, 17; Bettmann/Getty Images, 19; Rich Clarkson/NCAA Photos/Getty Images, 20–21, 28–29, 36–37; Elsa/Getty Images Sport/Getty Images, 22; Streeter Lecka/Getty Images Sport/Getty Images, 25; Gregory Shamus/Getty Images Sport/Getty Images, 27; Getty Images Sport/Getty Images, 30; Jim Gund/Getty Images Sport/Getty Images, 33; AP Images, 39; Bob Galbraith/AP Images, 40; Ben Solomon/NCAA Photos/Getty Images, 42; C. Morgan Engel/NCAA Photos/Getty Images, 44; Jonathan Daniel/Getty Images Sport/Getty Images, 45

Editor: Dalton Rains
Series Designer: Ebonee Estrella

Library of Congress Control Number: 2025939125

Publisher's Cataloging-in-Publication Data

Names: Beattie, Charlie, author.
Title: Unforgettable moments in March Madness / by Charlie Beattie
Description: Minneapolis, Minnesota: Abdo Publishing, 2026 | Series: Best of March Madness | Includes online resources and index.
Identifiers: ISBN 9781098298210 (lib. bdg.) | ISBN 9798384932017 (ebook)
Subjects: LCSH: Basketball--Juvenile literature. | College sports--Juvenile literature. | Basketball--Tournaments--United States--Juvenile literature. | College sports--United States--History--Juvenile literature. | NCAA Basketball Tournament--Juvenile literature. | March Madness (National Collegiate Athletic Association)--Juvenile literature.
Classification: DDC 796.32363--dc23

TABLE OF CONTENTS

22
LSU
10
SEC

CHAPTER ONE

THREE-POINT THROWDOWN

On April 1, 2024, two teams squared off in one of the most anticipated rematches in basketball history. The Louisiana State University (LSU) Tigers faced the Iowa Hawkeyes. The two teams were meeting in the Elite Eight of the women's National Collegiate Athletic Association (NCAA) Tournament.

Angel Reese, a physical 6-foot-3 forward, led LSU. Meanwhile, Iowa's offense was powered by the sharpshooting Caitlin Clark. The 6-foot guard had become one of the most recognizable basketball players of all time. One year earlier, Reese and Clark had met in the national championship game. Reese's Tigers won 102–85. Now the two seniors were meeting again, this time with a spot in the Final Four on the line.

Iowa guard Caitlin Clark (22) averaged 30.0 points per game in the 2024 women's NCAA Tournament.

Forward Angel Reese (10) celebrates during LSU's 2023 women's NCAA championship victory.

SETTING THE TONE

Just 17 seconds into the game, Clark dribbled around a screen set by forward Hannah Stuelke. Finding open space, Clark drilled a three-point shot. That gave the Hawkeyes a 3–0 lead. It also set a record. With the make, Clark passed legendary University of Connecticut (UConn) star Diana Taurasi for the most career three-pointers in NCAA Tournament history. But the Iowa star was just getting started.

Clark had entered the game with 531 career three-pointers. She was six short of the all-time record. Even for a great shooter, hitting six three-pointers in one game is a tall task. But Clark had made a career out of making the impossible look easy. In fact, she'd already posted 27 games with at least six three-pointers.

FIRING FROM DEEP

By the end of the first half, Clark had three makes from long-range and 15 total points. Each one of her triples came from far outside the three-point line. Clark stayed hot after the break. Just 11 seconds into the second half, she drained her fourth three-pointer. Soon, she added another. With 7:30 to go in the third quarter, Clark took a few dribbles past midcourt and pulled up for another shot

RECORD RATINGS

The 2023 women's championship game between Iowa and LSU was the most-watched women's basketball game ever. The numbers peaked at 12.6 million viewers. The rematch in the 2024 Elite Eight drew an even bigger audience. It peaked at 16 million viewers.

well beyond the arc. The ball splashed through the net and tied the record.

Reese and the Tigers weren't giving up. The teams had traded the lead throughout the game. Midway through the third quarter, Clark and the Hawkeyes had a chance to

Clark went 9-for-20 from three-point range in the 2024 Elite Eight.

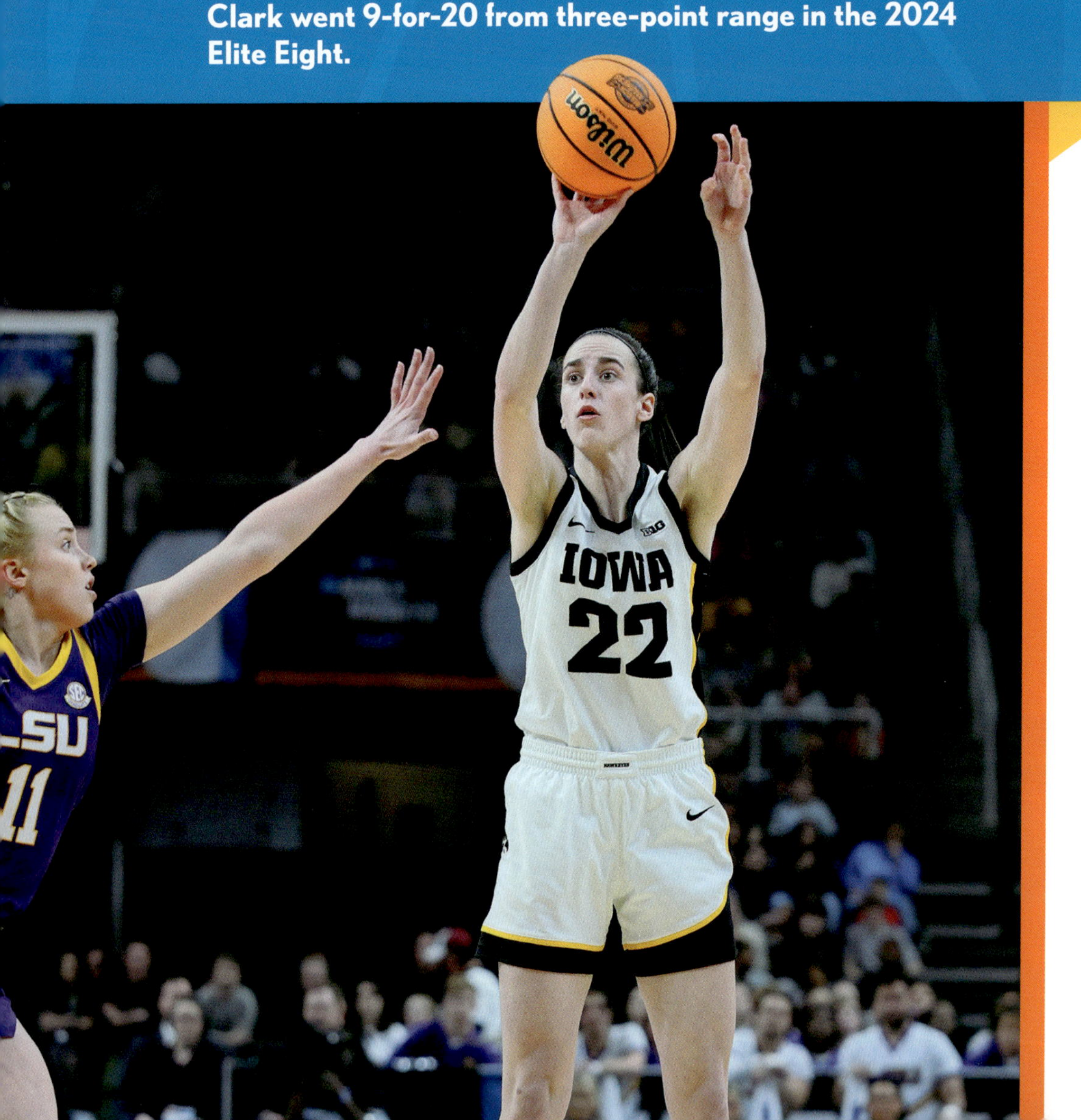

pull away. With Iowa leading by six, Clark darted around a teammate's screen, caught a pass, and tried to curl into the lane. Reese cut her off. So the Iowa guard dribbled back outside the three-point line. Reese extended an arm as Clark rose into the air. The record-breaking shot arced over LSU's three-time all-conference defender and dropped in the basket for a 61–52 Iowa lead. Reese could only hang her head in frustration as she jogged back up the floor.

THE DAGGER

Clark added another three-pointer early in the fourth quarter. Then she stepped back from defender Hailey Van Lith and drilled her ninth long-range make with 4:59 remaining. The shot tied the women's NCAA Tournament record for three-pointers made in a game. It also matched Clark's career high. But most importantly, it put Iowa up by 11. That proved too much for Reese and LSU to overcome.

Though Reese ended with 17 points and a game-high 20 rebounds, Clark's historic performance won the day. Behind her 41 points and 12 assists, the Hawkeyes won 94–87. Iowa's quest for a first national championship continued for another day. Clark and Reese had added two more unforgettable performances to the history of March Madness.

RAZORBACK
24
ZORBACKS
20

CHAPTER TWO

EARLY ROUND MADNESS

Saint Joseph's point guard Bryan Warrick grabbed a rebound and raced up the court in the second round of the 1981 men's NCAA Tournament. Less than 10 seconds remained. With two quick moves, he escaped a pair of DePaul defenders. Then he flung the ball to forward Lonnie McFarlan in the right corner. McFarlan flicked another quick pass to fellow forward John Smith, who stood underneath the basket. With a last-second layup, Smith lifted the No. 9 seed Hawks over No. 1 DePaul 49–48.

A few hours later, Arkansas guard U. S. Reed made a half-court shot to beat No. 4 Louisville 74–73. Soon after, No. 8 Kansas State's Rolando Blackman hit a baseline jumper to beat No. 2 Oregon State

Arkansas guards U. S. Reed, *left*, and Darrell Walker, *right*, celebrate Reed's buzzer-beater in the 1981 men's NCAA Tournament.

50–48. All three games aired on the same channel. Viewers were whisked from one thrilling finish to the next. For many, the term "March Madness" was born that day.

OPENING ROUND MOMENTS

In 1981, the men's field featured only 48 teams. But the opening rounds were still packed with close games. The NCAA Tournaments continued to grow more popular and eventually expanded to include 64 teams. That meant 32 first-round games were played in both the men's and the women's tournaments, creating even more opportunities for upsets and buzzer-beaters.

In 1998, the No. 13 seed Valparaiso Crusaders took on No. 4 Mississippi in the first round of the men's tournament. The Crusaders were coached by veteran Homer Drew, whose son Bryce starred on the team. A 6-foot-2 guard, Bryce Drew had scored 19 points as the Crusaders battled the Rebels down to the final moments of regulation.

Down 69–67 with less than 20 seconds to go, the Crusaders grabbed a rebound off a Mississippi miss. At the other end of the court, Drew got the ball off a give-and-go handoff and rose for a three-point shot. The ball clanked off the front of the rim. Mississippi forward Ansu Sesay grabbed the rebound, and Valparaiso was forced to foul with four seconds left. However, Sesay missed his two free throws, and the Crusaders got another chance.

This time, Jamie Sykes, who had been a minor league baseball player, started the play with the inbounds pass. He chucked the ball toward the opposite three-point line. Leaping over two defenders, forward Bill Jenkins managed to grab the pass and tip the ball to Bryce Drew, who was running down the sideline. Drew pulled up and launched a long jumper. The buzzer-beating shot fell

Valparaiso guard Bryce Drew averaged 20.7 points per game in the 1997–98 men's NCAA Tournament.

through the net. Valparaiso players flooded the court to celebrate the 70–69 win.

NORTHERN IOWA'S WILD WEEKEND

The first weekend at the NCAA Tournament moves fast. A team that wins its first-round game plays its next game two days later. In 2016, the University of Northern Iowa (UNI) men's team learned just how chaotic those first two rounds can be.

In the first round, the No. 11 Panthers led No. 6 Texas by two points with 2.6 seconds left. Then Longhorns guard Isaiah Taylor hit a running jumper to tie the game 72–72. In that kind of situation, coaches often take a timeout so they can draw up a final play. But UNI's coach let senior Matt Bohannon heave an inbounds pass to 6-foot-6 guard Paul Jesperson near the right sideline.

Jesperson took one dribble, bringing him just shy of midcourt. Then he flung the ball toward the basket. The 50-foot (15-m) shot was still in the air when the final buzzer sounded. A red outline appeared on the backboard as the ball banked into the net. It was the longest buzzer-beater in the history of either NCAA Tournament. Jesperson raised his arms in the air as teammates swarmed around him.

UNI faced No. 3 Texas A&M next. The Panthers silenced Aggies fans by building a double-digit lead late

UNI players celebrate after winning in the first round of the 2016 men's NCAA Tournament.

in the first half. They were still up 69-57 with 44 seconds to play. Then a Texas A&M layup cut the lead to 10. The Aggies' relentless full-court press caused UNI to fumble the inbounds pass and give up another quick score.

Now up by eight with 25.8 seconds remaining, Jesperson received the inbounds pass. Two defenders trapped the guard near the baseline and caused him to turn the ball over under the basket. The lead was down to six. On the Panthers' next inbounds play, guard Wyatt Lohaus threw the ball out of bounds. Texas A&M then scored a quick three-pointer to make it 69-66.

Finally making a successful inbounds pass, UNI got an easy dunk and pushed the lead back to five. But then Texas A&M guard Alex Caruso made a layup and was fouled. Caruso hit his free throw, cutting the lead to two.

After the next inbounds pass, Aggies defenders once again trapped the Panthers near the baseline. This time, guard Wes Washpun turned the ball over, and Texas A&M hit a layup with 1.9 seconds left.

Aggies fans let out a deafening cheer as the game-tying shot dropped in. Their team had made the biggest last-minute comeback in NCAA Tournament history. But the game wasn't over. After a neck-and-neck first overtime period, the Aggies pulled away in double overtime to win 92–88 and complete the massive comeback.

ANOTHER AGGIE COMEBACK

In 2017, the No. 5 seed Texas A&M women trailed No. 12 Pennsylvania 58–37. Then the Aggies pulled off a record-setting rally. Center Khaalia Hillsman finished the game with 27 points. She made a layup with 19.1 seconds left that put Texas A&M up 60–59. The Aggies never trailed again, winning 63–61 to complete the largest comeback in women's NCAA Tournament history.

Khaalia Hillsman grabbed nine rebounds in the first round of the 2017 women's NCAA Tournament.

MARATHON MATCHUP

In 1995, No. 4 Alabama and No. 5 Duke met in the second round of the women's NCAA Tournament. In the final seconds of regulation, Crimson Tide guard Niesa Johnson knocked down a three-pointer to tie the game 81–81 and force overtime.

The teams remained deadlocked through one overtime, and then through two more extra periods. In the fourth overtime, fouls became a problem for both teams. Two Blue Devils fouled out. Meanwhile, Johnson had been playing with four fouls since late in the second half.

By the closing seconds of the fourth overtime, the marathon game had dragged on for nearly three hours. But Johnson managed to stay on the court. With less than 10 seconds left, she hit two free throws to push the Crimson Tide's lead to four points. It was barely enough. Duke hit a three-pointer at the buzzer as Alabama held on for a 121–120 victory. Johnson recorded 28 points and helped the Crimson Tide win the longest and highest-scoring game in women's NCAA Tournament history.

IN THE CLUTCH

With one second left in the 1990 men's Sweet 16, UConn trailed Clemson by one point. Then UConn guard Scott Burrell heaved an inbounds pass nearly the entire length of the court. Fellow guard Tate George caught it and hit a spinning baseline jumper to win the game 71–70.

George's game-winner became known as "The Shot" to UConn fans. But just two days later, the Huskies were in another tight game in the Elite Eight. This time, UConn led Duke 78–77 in overtime. With 2.6 seconds left, George nearly stole a pass to seal the win. But it glanced off his hands and went out of bounds. Christian Laettner inbounded the ball to a Duke teammate, who gave the ball right back to Laettner. The 6-foot-11 center hit an off-balance shot to win the game.

In 1992, defending-champion Duke faced Kentucky in another Elite Eight classic. The game stretched into overtime as the teams battled for a spot in the Final Four. With 2.1 seconds left in the extra period, Kentucky guard

Center Christian Laettner (32) posted 23 points in Duke's 1990 Elite Eight victory over UConn.

Sean Woods hit a bank shot. That put the Wildcats up 103–102. Blue Devils coach Mike Krzyzewski called a timeout to set up a play. He wanted Laettner to take the last shot. Grant Hill, the team's star forward, threw a perfect strike on the inbounds pass. Catching the ball at the opposite free-throw line, Laettner turned and released a jumper. It dropped through the hoop as time expired, sending the Blue Devils back to the Final Four and a second straight title run.

54
ARQUETTE
33

CHAPTER THREE

FINAL FOUR MOMENTS

With five seconds left in regulation, Charlotte forward Cedric Maxwell hit a jump shot. Charlotte was facing Marquette in the 1977 men's Final Four. The basket tied the game at 49–49. After a timeout, Marquette guard Butch Lee heaved a baseball pass to the opposite foul line. Lee's teammate, 6-foot-10 center Jerome Whitehead, snatched it away from a defender. Whitehead then turned and powered to the basket. He hit a shot just as the buzzer sounded.

For a moment, fans weren't sure the game was over. After a delay, officials ruled that Whitehead's last-second shot was good. Marquette won the game 51–49. Two days later, the school captured its first national title.

Marquette forward Jerome Whitehead (54) scored 21 points in the 1977 men's Final Four.

Tennessee point guard Tasha Butts, *right*, averaged 10.5 points and 7.3 rebounds per game in the 2004 women's NCAA Tournament.

STEAL AND SCORE

In 2004, Tasha Butts powered Tennessee through a deep run in the women's NCAA tournament. One clutch moment happened in the Sweet 16. The Lady Vols point guard drained two free throws with 0.2 seconds left to beat Baylor 71–69. Two days later, Butts was the hero again. She scored a late basket to help Tennessee beat Stanford 62–60.

The Lady Vols next traveled to New Orleans, Louisiana, for a Final Four matchup with conference-rival LSU. The Tigers were playing close to home, but Tennessee battled through the noise of LSU fans' jeers and kept the game close. With 20 seconds left, the score was 50–50. Butts had a chance for another last-second game-winner, but her shot fell short. The Lady Vols knocked the ball out of bounds after a battle for the rebound.

With six seconds left, LSU inbounded the ball to Temeka Johnson. The Tigers star point guard was quickly double-teamed. While trying to split the Lady Vols defenders, Johnson slipped and lost the ball. Tennessee forward Shyra Ely scooped it up and flipped a pass to fellow forward LaToya Davis, who was alone underneath the basket. Davis laid in the winning shot.

FREE-THROW FINISH

Virginia entered the 2019 men's Final Four with the nation's best defense. The Cavaliers had allowed just 56.1 points per game that season. For the first 35 minutes of the semifinal matchup, that defense held Auburn to

47 points. The Cavaliers just had to hold on to their 10-point lead for a few more minutes.

But Virginia's shooters went cold. To make things worse, Auburn kept hitting shots. The Tigers scored the next 14 points and took the lead. With 7.4 seconds left, the Cavaliers finally made another basket. A three-pointer from Kyle Guy cut Auburn's lead to 61–60.

Virginia fouled Auburn's Jared Harper immediately after the inbounds pass, sending the guard to the free-throw line. Harper drained his first shot, but his next attempt clanked off the rim. Virginia grabbed the board.

Two fouls from Auburn drained a few more seconds off the clock. Then the Cavaliers called timeout. They got ready to inbound with 1.5 seconds on the clock. Fans throughout the arena were on their feet as they waited for the final play.

Guy received the inbounds pass in the left corner and hoisted up a three-pointer. His shot was short, but an Auburn defender fouled him during the shot. That put Guy on the line for the three most important free throws of his career.

Guy's first shot was good, cutting the lead to one. His second tied the game 62–62. Auburn called a timeout after that. They wanted Guy to think about the third shot and feel the pressure. Finally, Guy stepped back to the line. Virginia fans held their breath, and Auburn fans jeered loudly. But the clutch free throw dropped through the net. The Cavaliers took a one-point lead.

Auburn still had 0.6 seconds left. The Tigers hurled a long inbounds pass to guard Bryce Brown, who sent a twisting shot toward the rim. It came up short, and Virginia's bench stormed the court to celebrate the 63–62 win. Two days later, the Cavaliers beat Texas Tech

Virginia guard Kyle Guy (5) is fouled on a last-second three-point try during the 2019 men's Final Four.

85-77 in overtime to capture the program's first national championship.

BUZZER-BEATER

Florida Atlantic led the San Diego State Aztecs by 14 points early in the second half of the 2023 men's Final Four. It was the first appearance in the national semifinals for either team. The Owls appeared ready to roll on to their first championship game. Then the Aztecs began chipping away at the lead.

Florida Atlantic's lead was cut to 71-70 with nine seconds left. Then San Diego State center Nathan

SUGGS'S SHOT

The 2020 NCAA Tournaments were canceled due to the COVID-19 pandemic. When the Final Four returned in 2021, Gonzaga's Jalen Suggs reminded fans everywhere just how exciting March Madness could be. Suggs's Bulldogs were tied with the University of California, Los Angeles (UCLA), with just 3.3 seconds remaining in overtime. The Gonzaga point guard grabbed an inbounds pass and sprinted up the floor. He heaved up a shot just past midcourt. It banked into the hoop, sending the Bulldogs to the championship game.

San Diego State guard Lamont Butler, *far right*, takes a shot as time expires in the 2023 Men's Final Four.

Mensah grabbed a rebound and quickly got the ball to guard Lamont Butler. The 6-foot-2 junior sprinted toward the basket. But a Florida Atlantic defender cut him off. With two seconds left, Butler hoisted up a jump shot. It dropped through the hoop as time expired. The Aztecs won 72–71.

Before Butler, no player had hit a buzzer-beating game-winner when their team was behind. The Aztecs ultimately fell short of a championship, losing 76–59 to UConn two days later. But the Final Four game-winner was already cemented into NCAA Tournament history.

23
C.SMITH
32

CHAPTER FOUR

CHAMPIONSHIP MOMENTS

North Carolina inbounded the ball with 32 seconds left in the 1982 men's national championship. The Tar Heels trailed Georgetown 62–61. They passed the ball around looking for the right opening.

Then freshman Michael Jordan got open on the left wing. He drilled a go-ahead shot with 16 seconds to go. North Carolina clinched the national title after a defensive stop on Georgetown's next possession.

A year after Jordan's iconic shot, a lesser-known player made one that was just as impressive. The Houston Cougars were big favorites against NC State in the 1983 title game. But with 44 seconds left, the score was 52–52. The Wolfpack had the ball.

Michael Jordan (23) takes the game-winning shot in the 1982 men's NCAA championship game.

Head coach Jim Valvano celebrates with players after NC State's victory in the 1983 men's NCAA championship game.

Since the NCAA had no shot clock at the time, the underdogs could hold for the final shot.

Among the five NC State players on the floor, forward Lorenzo Charles was a last resort on offense. Not a single pass went his way in the Wolfpack's final possession. Finally, with three seconds left, star guard Dereck Whittenburg launched a long jumper. It fell short. Thinking fast, Charles grabbed the ball and slammed down a dunk as time expired. Coach Jim Valvano ran onto the court in joyful disbelief. NC State's unlikely hero had clinched an improbable championship win.

THE ILL-TIMED TIMEOUT

Some championship moments create instant heroes. But a player's legacy can also be affected by a mistake. In 1993, Michigan's Chris Webber learned that the hard way.

By the time the Michigan Wolverines reached the 1993 men's national championship, they were one of the most well-known basketball teams in the world. Forwards Chris Webber and Ray Jackson, guards Jimmy King and Jalen Rose, and center Juwan Howard emerged as Michigan's starting lineup as freshmen in 1991–92. "The Fab Five" played with flair and confidence. They also changed basketball fashion by wearing baggy shorts. Fans either loved or hated the group. But everyone wanted to see them play.

The Wolverines had lost to Duke in the 1992 NCAA title game. A year later, they trailed North Carolina 73–71 with 19 seconds left. Then Webber grabbed a rebound off a missed Tar Heels free throw.

Webber raced up the floor. But he got trapped by two defenders. Panicking, Webber signaled for a timeout with 11 seconds remaining. Michigan didn't have any left. By rule, Webber had committed a technical foul. North Carolina was awarded two free throws and possession of the ball. The Tar Heels won 77–71. Decades later, Webber's blunder was still remembered as one of the biggest mistakes in NCAA Tournament history.

GAME WINNERS

In 1994, North Carolina took on Louisiana Tech in the women's national championship. Guard Pam Thomas hit a long jump shot with 16 seconds left. It put the Lady Techsters up 59–57.

North Carolina missed a potential game-tying shot. But the Tar Heels came up with the ball after a battle for the rebound. With 0.7 seconds on the clock, head coach Sylvia Hatchell called timeout to set up one last play.

Hatchell first designed a lob play. But the Lady Techsters covered the lane well. Hatchell had to call another timeout. She designed a new play. This time, she hoped Charlotte Smith could get open at the three-point line. It was a risky play. Smith wasn't known as a three-point shooter. But the forward was able to grab the inbounds pass and knock down the title-winning shot.

More than two decades passed before fans witnessed another buzzer-beater in an NCAA championship game.

BUZZER-BEATING BLOCK

With seconds to play in the 2003 men's title game, Syracuse led Kansas 81–78. Kansas guard Michael Lee got open on the left wing and attempted a potential game-tying three-pointer. But Syracuse sophomore forward Hakim Warrick got a hand on the shot. The block helped seal Syracuse's first national championship.

Charlotte Smith posted 20 points and 23 rebounds in the 1994 women's NCAA championship game.

This time, North Carolina's men's team was involved. Facing Villanova in the 2016 final, the Tar Heels were down by 10 with under five minutes to play. But they fought back. Guard Marcus Paige hit a game-tying three with 4.7 seconds left.

Villanova took its final timeout. Coach Jay Wright called a play that the Wildcats had practiced all year. Point guard Ryan Arcidiacono received an inbounds pass from Kris Jenkins. Then Jenkins trailed behind as the guard raced up the floor. When Arcidiacono reached the three-point line, he shoveled a pass back to the forward. Jenkins hit a deep three-pointer just as the final buzzer sounded, and Villanova clinched the championship.

TWO-TIME HERO

UConn rode a 111-game winning streak into the 2017 women's Final Four. Most fans expected the Huskies to add to the streak and march to a fourth straight title. Instead, with time expiring in overtime, Mississippi State guard Morgan William sank a tiebreaking shot.

One year later, the Huskies found themselves in another Final-Four nail-biter. This time, Notre Dame guard Arike Ogunbowale hit a step-back jump shot with one second left to beat UConn 91–89. The shot sent Notre Dame to a title-game matchup against William and Mississippi State.

Ogunbowale struggled for most of the game. She hit only five of her first 20 shots. Even so, with the game tied 58–58 and three seconds left, Fighting Irish coach Muffet McGraw didn't hesitate to call a play for her star player.

Notre Dame inbounded from the right wing. Ogunbowale fought through the crowd of defenders to take a short pass. She then peeled down the wing and heaved up an off-balance three-pointer. It went in as time expired. The shot gave Notre Dame its first title in 17 years and cemented Ogunbowale's name in tournament lore.

Arike Ogunbowale (24) releases a game-winning buzzer-beater in the 2018 women's NCAA championship.

STATE
22
33
15
STATE
41

CHAPTER FIVE

INSPIRATIONAL MOMENTS

In the early days of the men's NCAA Tournament, college basketball was a racially segregated sport. Although most of the country began to change racist rules through the 1950s and early 1960s, some universities in the South still held out. Mississippi State was one of those schools.

In 1963, the Bulldogs' all-white team was set to face Loyola University Chicago in the second round of the men's tournament in Lansing, Michigan. But the Ramblers had four Black starters. If Mississippi State traveled to the game, the team would be breaking what was known as an "unwritten" law in Mississippi against integrated sports.

Even so, Bulldogs coach James McCarthy snuck his team out of the state. Loyola won 61–51 on its way

Forward Jerry Harkness (15) scored 20 points in Loyola's victory over Mississippi State in the 1963 men's NCAA Tournament.

to a national championship. But many people remember the team's second-round matchup as much as the final. It became known as "The Game of Change."

But many coaches still held racist beliefs about Black players. They thought that a team could not succeed without at least one white starter. In 1966, Texas Western reached the national championship. For the first time, five Black players started the title game. Led by 20 points from point guard Bobby Joe Hill, Texas Western beat an all-white Kentucky team 72–65. The historic win helped take down racist assumptions and nudge college basketball forward.

LEADING THE WAY

Despite small steps forward, Black coaches still had few job opportunities. In 1982, John Thompson of Georgetown became the first Black coach to reach the Final Four. That year, the Hoyas lost a close matchup with North Carolina.

Two years later, Thompson led the Hoyas back to the title game. This time, they faced Houston. Thompson's team won 84–75. Afterward, media members tried to highlight the fact that Thompson was the first Black coach to win a title. Thompson, who had always been a strong advocate for civil rights, wouldn't accept the attention. He said he was proud to win. However, the fact that he had

Head coach John Thompson, *left*, and center Patrick Ewing, *right*, celebrate Georgetown's victory in the 1982 men's national championship.

made history just proved that Black coaches before him never received the chance they deserved.

A UNIQUE TRIBUTE

In the late 1980s, Loyola Marymount built a reputation as an offensive powerhouse. Lions players sprinted up the court on every possession, hoping to score as quickly as possible. In 1989–90, the team led the nation by averaging 122.4 points per game.

However, the small California school suffered a devastating tragedy. Star forward Hank Gathers had been diagnosed with a heart condition during the season. In the semifinals of the West Coast Conference (WCC)

Tournament, the 6-foot-7 senior collapsed on the court. He died a short time later.

The WCC Tournament was canceled. But the Lions were awarded the conference's NCAA Tournament spot. Loyola Marymount went against New Mexico State in the first round. Early in the second half, the Lions' other star, guard Bo Kimble, was fouled. The right-handed Kimble placed the ball in his left hand and made his first free throw. The shot was a tribute to Gathers, who had shot free throws with his left hand.

Kimble continued the tribute. He shot his first free throw of each game left-handed. The No. 11 Lions upset

Loyola guard Bo Kimble (30) averaged 35.8 points per game in the 1990 men's NCAA Tournament.

three higher-seeded teams and made a Cinderella run to the Elite Eight.

SISTER JEAN

More than five decades after Loyola University Chicago's 1963 run, the Ramblers qualified for the 2018 field as a No. 11 seed. Few people outside of the school knew about the team's biggest fan. Her name was Sister Jean Dolores Schmidt, a nun who had been the Ramblers' team chaplain since 1994. The 98-year-old watched every game from her wheelchair near the team bench. In 2018, the Ramblers survived three close games to start the tournament. Loyola became the first No. 11 seed to reach the Final Four in 12 years.

TV cameras often focused on Sister Jean. Fans got to see her reaction after every big play. They discovered that she had a pair of custom basketball shoes. Her left shoe had *Sister* stitched into the heel. Her right shoe read *Jean*. Viewers also learned that she prayed with the team before every game, sometimes asking for a Loyola win or for a fairly called game by the officials.

Loyola fell to Michigan in the Final Four. But when the Ramblers returned to the tournament in 2021, Sister Jean was back. Now 101 years old, the nun watched as No. 8 seed Loyola upset No. 1 seed Illinois in the second round.

MILESTONE MATCHUPS

The women's NCAA Tournament debuted in 1982. For decades, it struggled to draw fans. Even in 2022, when a record 4.85 million fans watched on television as South Carolina beat UConn for the women's title, the men's final gathered three times as many viewers.

The next season, two women's stars captured America's attention. Iowa's high-scoring guard, Caitlin Clark, thrilled audiences with her long-range shooting. LSU's Angel Reese was a bold player who sometimes

Caitlin Clark, *left*, scored 30 points in the 2024 women's NCAA championship game.

taunted opponents. That made her a controversial star. But she backed up her talk with spectacular all-around play.

Clark and Reese met in the 2023 championship game. Millions tuned in to watch LSU beat Iowa 102–85. A year later, Clark carried the Hawkeyes back to the title game. They faced an undefeated South Carolina team. Once again, the game attracted scores of fans. More than 18 million watched as the Gamecocks completed their perfect season with an 87–75 win.

NEW HEIGHTS

Many people compared the 2023 NCAA women's championship game to a title-game matchup that happened more than 40 years earlier. On March 26, 1979, Michigan State and Indiana State drew 35 million television viewers. Earvin "Magic" Johnson's Spartans beat Larry Bird's Sycamores 75–64. Nearly 50 years later, it was still the most-watched college basketball game ever. The popularity of that game helped the NCAA Tournament grow into one of the nation's top sporting events.

While massive viewer growth was impressive, it was far from the only surprise. When the ratings for the men's final came out, they revealed that 14.82 million fans had tuned in to watch UConn beat Purdue. The women had drawn more fans than the men for the first time ever.

HONORABLE MENTIONS

UTAH VS. DARTMOUTH—
1944 MEN'S CHAMPIONSHIP

The men's NCAA Tournament was only five years old in 1944. Utah and Dartmouth were tied 40–40 with three seconds left in overtime of the title game. Utes forward Herb Wilkinson then hit a shot as time expired. It was the first buzzer-beater in any NCAA Tournament game.

PRINCETON VS. WICHITA STATE—
1965 MEN'S THIRD-PLACE GAME

Princeton lost to Michigan in the 1965 men's Final Four, but Bill Bradley saved his best performance for the third-place game, played by the two semifinals losers. The 6-foot-5 forward torched Wichita State with 58 points. The third-place game was removed from the tournament after 1981. But Bradley still held the Final Four record 60 years after he set it.

MARYLAND VS. DUKE—
2006 WOMEN'S CHAMPIONSHIP

Maryland trailed Duke 70–67 in the final 10 seconds of the 2006 women's title game. Kristi Toliver, a 5-foot-7 guard, knocked down a game-tying three-pointer. The shot forced overtime, and the Terrapins went on to win the game 78–75.

Paige Bueckers

Gordon Hayward

BUTLER VS. DUKE— 2010 MEN'S CHAMPIONSHIP

No. 5 seed Butler was a huge underdog against No. 1 Duke in the 2010 men's title game. But the Bulldogs kept it close. They were within two points at 61–59 with 3.6 seconds left. Butler forward Gordon Hayward grabbed a rebound off a missed Duke free throw. His half-court shot bounced off the backboard and the rim, inches away from a miracle finish.

HOUSTON VS. FLORIDA— 2025 MEN'S CHAMPIONSHIP

Houston had trailed Duke 66–59 with 1:14 remaining in the 2025 men's Final Four. The Cougars went on an 11–1 run to pull off a stunning 70–67 win. In the championship against Florida, the tables turned. Houston let a 12-point second-half lead slip away. The Gators won 70–67.

UCONN—2025 WOMEN'S CHAMPIONSHIP

Point guard Paige Bueckers arrived at UConn in 2020 as one of the nation's top players. But she struggled with injuries over the next few seasons. In 2025, she finally led the Huskies to a title. With UConn up 82–53 in the championship game against South Carolina, Coach Geno Auriemma benched Bueckers so she could get an ovation as she left the court. The senior guard and head coach shared an emotional hug as the crowd cheered.

GLOSSARY

assist
A pass that leads directly to a basket.

baseline
The out-of-bounds line underneath each basket, along the short sides of the court.

chaplain
A person who performs religious work for a hospital, school, prison, or military.

integrated
Including people of different races, genders, ethnicities, or other factors.

overtime
An extra period of play when the score is tied after regulation.

pandemic
A widespread outbreak of a disease that affects a large portion of the population.

ratings
Statistics used to measure how many people are watching a television show.

rival
An opponent with whom a player or team has a fierce and ongoing competition.

screen
A legal block made by an offensive player against a defender to open up a teammate for a shot or a pass.

seed
A rank assigned to a player or team in a tournament.

segregated
Kept apart based on race, gender, ethnicity, or other factors.

trap
A play in which two or more defenders close in on the ball to try to force a turnover.

tribute
An act carried out to honor someone.

underdog
The person or team that is not expected to win.

MORE INFORMATION

BOOKS

Big Book of Who Women in Sports: The 101 Stars Every Fan Needs to Know. Triumph, 2025.

Giedd, Steph. *Basketball Strategies.* Abdo, 2024.

Hanlon, Luke. *Caitlin Clark.* Abdo, 2025.

ONLINE RESOURCES

To learn more about unforgettable March Madness moments, please visit **abdobooklinks.com** or scan this QR code. These links are routinely monitored and updated to provide the most current information available.

INDEX

ABOUT THE AUTHOR

Charlie Beattie is a writer, editor, and former sportscaster. Originally from Saint Paul, Minnesota, he now lives in Charleston, South Carolina, with his wife and son.